P9-DNQ-593

COACH

COACH

LESSONS ON THE GAME OF LIFE

MICHAEL

LEWIS

W. W. NORTON & COMPANY

New York   London

For information about permission to reproduce selections from this book,
write to Permissions, W. W. Norton & Company, Inc.,
500 Fifth Avenue, New York, NY 10110

Manufacturing by R.R. Donnelley, Bloomsburg, PA
Book design by JAM Design
Production manager: Andrew Marasia

Library of Congress Cataloging-in-Publication Data

Lewis, Michael (Michael M.)
Coach : lessons on the game of life / Michael Lewis.—1st ed.
p. cm.
ISBN 0-393-06091-8 (hardcover)
1. Baseball coaches—Louisiana—New Orleans—Anecdotes. 2. Lewis,
Michael (Michael M.)—Childhood and youth. 3. Conduct of life. I. Title.
GV873.L49 2005
796.323'092—dc22

2004026048

W. W. Norton & Company, Inc.
500 Fifth Avenue, New York, N.Y. 10110
www.wwnorton.com

W. W. Norton & Company Ltd.
Castle House, 75/76 Wells Street, London W1T 3QT

1 2 3 4 5 6 7 8 9 0

FOR QUINN AND DIXIE

WHEN I was twelve I thought that when the New Orleans *Times-Picayune* ran a headline about the "struggle for control of the West Bank" it meant the other side of the Mississippi River. I thought that my shiny gold velour pants actually looked good. I kept a giant sack of Nabisco Chocolate Chip cookies under my bed so that they might be available in an emergency—a flood, say, or a hurricane—that made it harder to get to the grocery store. From the safe distance of forty-three, "twelve" looks less an age than a disease, and, for the most part, I've been able to forget all about it—not the events and the people, but the feelings that gave them meaning. But there are exceptions. A few people, and a few experiences, simply refuse to be trivialized by time. There are teachers with a rare ability to enter a child's mind; it's as if their ability to get there at all gives them the right to stay forever. I'd once had such a teacher. His name was Billy Fitzgerald, but everybody just called him Coach Fitz.

Forgetting Fitz was impossible—I'll come to why in a moment—but avoiding him should have been a breeze. And for nearly thirty years I'd had next to nothing to do with him, or with the school where he'd coached me, the Isidore Newman School. But in just the past year, I heard two pieces of news about him that, taken together, made him sound suspiciously like something I never imagined he could be: a mystery. The first came last spring, when one of his former players, a forty-four-year-old New Orleans financier named David Pointer, had the idea of redoing the old school's gym, and naming it for Coach

Fitz. Pointer started calling around and found that hundreds of former players and their parents shared his enthusiasm for his old coach, and the money poured in. "The most common response from the parents," said Pointer, "is that Fitz did all the hard work."

Then came the second piece of news: during the summer baseball season, Fitz had given a speech to his current Newman players. It had been a long, depressing season: the kids, who during the school year had won the Louisiana state baseball championship, had lost interest. Fitz had grown increasingly upset with them until, after their final game, he'd gone around the room and explained what was wrong with each and every one of them. One player had skipped practice and lied about why; another blamed everyone but himself for his failure; a third had wasted his talent to pursue a life of ease; a fourth had agreed before the summer to lose fifteen pounds and instead gained ten. The players went home and complained about Fitz to their parents. Fathers of eight of them—half the baseball team—had then complained to the headmaster. Several of them wanted Fitz fired.

The past was no longer on speaking terms with the present. As the cash poured in from former players, and parents of former players, who wanted to name the gym for Fitz, his current players, and their parents, were doing their best to persuade the headmaster to get rid of him. I called a couple of the players involved, now college freshmen. Their fathers had been among the complainers, but they spoke of the episode as a kind of natural disaster beyond their control. One of them called his teammates "a bunch of whiners," and explained that the reason Fitz was in such trouble was that "a lot of the parents are big money donors."

I grew curious enough to fly down to New

Orleans to see the headmaster. The Isidore Newman School is the sort of small, wealthy private school that every midsized American city has at least two of—one of them called Country Day. Most of the seventy or so kids in my class came from families that were affluent by local standards. I'm not sure how many of us thought we'd hit a triple, but quite a few had been born on third base. The school's most striking trait was that it was founded in 1903 as a manual training school for Jewish orphans. About half of my classmates were Jewish, but I didn't know any orphans. In any case, the current headmaster's name was Scott McLeod, and, he said, the school he'd taken charge of in 1993 was different from the school I'd graduated from in 1978. "The parents' willingness to intercede on the kids' behalf, to take the kids' side, to protect the kid, in a not-healthy way—there's much more of that each year," he said. "It's true in sports, it's true in the classroom. And it's only going to get

worse." Fitz sat at the very top of the list of hardships that parents protected their kids from; indeed, the first angry call McLeod received after he became headmaster came from a father who was upset that Fitz wasn't giving his son more playing time.

Since then the beleaguered headmaster had been like a man in an earthquake straddling a fissure. On one side he had this coach about whom former players cared intensely; on the other side he had these newly organized and outraged parents of current players. When I asked him why he didn't simply ignore the parents, he said, quickly, that he couldn't do that: the parents were his customers. ("They pay a hefty tuition," he said. "That entitles them to a say.") But when I asked him if he'd ever thought about firing Coach Fitz, he had to think hard about it. "The parents want so much for their kids to have success as they define it," he said. "They want them to get into the best schools, and go on to the best jobs. And so if they see their kid fail—if he's only on the JV, or the coach is yelling at him—somehow the school is responsible for that." And while he didn't see how he could ever "fire a legend," he did see how he could change him. Several times in his tenure he had done something his predecessors never had done: summon Fitz to his office and insist that he "modify" his behavior. "And to his credit," the headmaster said, "he did that."

Obviously, whatever Fitz had done to modify his behavior hadn't satisfied his critics. But then, from where he started, he had a long way to go.

WHEN we first laid eyes on him, we had no idea who he was, except that he played in the Oakland A's farm system, and was spending his off-season, for reasons we couldn't fathom, coaching eighth-grade basketball. We were in the seventh grade, and so, theoretically, indifferent to his existence. But the outdoor court on which we seventh graders practiced was just an oak tree apart from the eighth grade's court. And within days of this new coach's arrival, we found ourselves riveted by his performance. Our coach was a pleasant, mild-mannered fellow, and our practices were always pleasant, mild-mannered affairs. The eighth grade's practices were something else: a 6'4", 220-pound minor league catcher with the face of a street fighter hollering at the top of his lungs for three straight hours. Often as not, the eighth graders had done something to offend their new coach's sensibilities, and he'd have them running wind sprints until they doubled over. When finally they collapsed, unable to run another step, he'd pull from his back pocket the collected works of Bobby Knight and begin reading aloud.

This was new. We didn't know what to make of it. Sean put it best. Sean was Sean Tuohy, our best player and, therefore, our authority on pretty much everything. That year he'd lead us to a 32–0 record; a few years later, he'd lead our high school to a pair of Louisiana state championships; and a few years after that he'd take Ole Miss to its first-ever SEC basketball title. He'd set the SEC record for career assists (he still holds it) and get himself drafted by the New Jersey Nets—not bad for a skinny six-foot white kid in a game yet to establish a three-point line. Sean Tuohy had fight enough in him for three. But one afternoon during seventh-grade basketball practice, Sean looked over at this bizarre parallel universe being created on the next court by this large, ferocious man and said, "Oh God, please don't ever let me get to the eighth grade."

AS it turned out, eighth grade was inevitable, though by the time we got to it Fitz had moved on to coach the high school. My own experience of him began the summer after my freshman year, after he quit the Oakland A's farm system and became the Newman

baseball and basketball coach. I was fourteen, could pass for twelve, and of no obvious athletic use. It was the last night of the season. We were tied for first place with our opponents. The stands were packed. Sean Tuohy was on the mound, it was the bottom of the last inning, and we were up 2–1. (These things you don't forget.) There was only one out, and the other team put runners on first and third, but, from my comfortable seat on the bench, it was hard to get too worked up about it. The luna moths jitterbugged in the stadium lights; the small children frolicked on the other side of the chain-link fence, waiting for foul balls; and there was no reason to believe this night would turn out any different than any other. The first rule of New Orleans life was that, whatever game he happened to be playing, Sean Tuohy won it. Then Fitz made his second trip of the inning to the pitcher's mound, and all hell broke loose in the stands. Their fans started hollering at the umps: it was illegal to visit the mound twice in one inning. The umpires, wary as ever of being caught listening to fans, were clearly inclined to overlook the whole matter. But before they could, a famous New Orleans high school baseball coach, who carried a rule book on his person, waddled out from the stands onto the field and stopped the game. Him, the umps had to listen to: Sean Tuohy had to be yanked.

Out of one side of his mouth Fitz tore into the high school coach with the rule book—who scurried, rat-like, back to the safety of his seat; out of the other he shouted at me to warm up. The ballpark was already in an uproar, but the sight of me (I resembled a scoop of vanilla ice cream, with four pick-up sticks jutting out from it) sent their side into spasms of delight. Even I was aware that there was something faintly incredible about me in that situation. I represented an extreme example of our team's general inability to intimidate the opposition. The other team's dugout needed a shave; ours needed, at most, a bath. (Some unwritten rule in male adolescence dictates that the lower your parents' tax bracket, the sooner you acquire facial hair.) As I walked out to the mound, their hairy, well-muscled players danced jigs in their dugout, their coaches high-fived, their fans celebrated and shouted lighthearted insults. The game, as far as they were concerned, was over. I might have been unnerved if I'd paid them any attention; but I was, at that moment, fixated on the only deeply frightening thing in the entire ballpark: Coach Fitz.

By then I had heard (from the eighth graders, I believe) all the Fitz stories. Billy Fitzgerald had been one of the best high school basketball and baseball players ever seen in New Orleans, and he'd gone on to play both sports at Tulane University. He'd been a first-round draft choice of the Oakland A's. He was, we assumed, destined for stardom in the big leagues. But we never discussed Fitz's accomplishments. We

were far more interested in his *intensity*. In high school, when his team lost, Fitz had refused to board the bus; he *walked*, in his catcher's gear, from the ballpark on one end of New Orleans to his home on the other. Back then he'd played against another New Orleans superstar, Rusty Staub. Staub, on second base, made the mistake of taunting Fitz's pitcher. Fitz raced out from behind home plate and, in full catcher's gear, chased the terrified future All-Star around the field. I'd heard another, similar story about Fitz and Pete Maravich, the basketball legend. When Fitz's Tulane team played Maravich's LSU team, Fitz, a tenacious defender, had naturally been assigned to guard Maravich. Pistol Pete had rung him up for 66 points, but before he'd finished, he too had made the mistake of taunting Fitz. It was, as the eighth graders put it, a two-hit fight: Fitz hit Pistol Pete, and Pistol Pete hit the floor. But it got better: Maravich's father, Press, happened to be the LSU basketball coach. When he saw Fitz deck his son, he'd run out and jumped on the pile. Fitz had made the cover of *Sports Illustrated*, with Pete in a headlock and Press on his back.

And now he was standing on the pitcher's mound, erupting with a Vesuvian fury, waiting for me to arrive. When I did, he handed me the ball and said, in effect, Put it where the sun don't shine. I looked at their players, hugging and mugging and dancing and jeering. No, they did not appear to suspect that I was going to put it anyplace unpleasant. Then Fitz leaned down, put his hand on my shoulder, and, thrusting his face right up to mine, became as calm as the eye of a storm. It was just him and me now; we were in this together. I have no idea where the man's intention ended and his instincts took over, but the effect of his performance was to say: *there's no one I'd rather have out here in this life-or-death situation.* And I believed him!

As the other team continued to erupt with glee,

Fitz glanced at their runner on third base, a reedy fellow with an aspiring mustache, and said, "Pick him off." Then he walked off and left me all alone.

If Zeus had landed on the pitcher's mound and issued the command, it would have had no greater impact. The chances of picking a man off third base are never good, and even worse in a close game, when everyone's paying attention. But this was Fitz talking; and I can still recall, thirty years later, the sensation he created in me. I didn't have words for it then, but I do now: *I am about to show the world, and myself, what I can do.*

At the time, this was a wholly novel thought for me. I'd spent the previous school year racking up C-minuses, picking fights with teachers, and thinking up new ways to waste my time on earth. Worst of all, I had the most admirable, loving parents, on whom I could plausibly blame nothing. What was wrong with me? I didn't know. To say I was "confused" would be

to put it kindly; "inert" would be closer to the truth. In the three years before I met Coach Fitz, the only task for which I exhibited any enthusiasm was sneaking out of the house at two in the morning to rip hood ornaments off cars—you needed a hacksaw and two full nights to cut the winged medallion off a Bentley. Now this fantastically persuasive man was insisting, however improbably, that I might be some other kind of person. A hero.

The kid with the fuzz on his upper lip bounced crazily off third base, oblivious to the fact that he represented a new solution to an adolescent life crisis. The ball was in the third baseman's glove before he knew what happened. He just flopped around in the dirt as our third baseman applied the tag. I struck out the next guy, and we won the game. Afterward, Coach Fitz called us together for a brief sermon. Hot with rage at the coach with the rule book—the ballpark still felt like it was about to explode—he told us all that there was a quality no one within five miles of this place even knew about, called "guts," that we all embodied. He threw me the game ball, and said he'd never in all his life seen such courage on the pitcher's mound. He'd caught Catfish Hunter and Rollie Fingers and a lot of other big league pitchers—but who were *they*?

A few weeks later, when school started again, I was told the headmaster wanted to see me in his office. I didn't need directions. (My most recent trip, a few months earlier, had come after I turned on an English teacher and asked, "Are you always so pleasant, or is this just an especially good day for you?") But this time the headmaster had surprising news. Fitz had just spoken to him, he said. There might be hope for me after all.

But there wasn't, yet. I had thought the point of this whole episode was simple: winning is everything.

———

I CONFESS that the current headmaster didn't clarify matters for me. Fitz had modified his behavior—he was, the headmaster agreed, mellower than ever—and yet his intensity was more loathed than ever. Anyway, his unmodified behavior is the reason his former players hoped to name the gym for him. The school had given me a list of people, most of whom I didn't know, who had played for Fitz. I had called up about twenty of them, to ask them how they felt now about the experience. I knew there must be people who never reconciled themselves to Fitz—who still didn't understand what he was trying to do for them—but they were hard to find. The collective response of Fitz's former players could be fairly summarized in a sentence: *Fitz changed my life.* All of them had their own favorite Fitz stories, and it's worth hearing at least one of them, to get their general flavor. Here is Philip Skelding, Rhodes

scholar and twenty-nine-year-old student at the Harvard Medical School, who played basketball for Fitz:

I wasn't a natural athlete—I had to work at it. I was the only starter whose scoring average was lower than his GPA. It was my junior year—the first year we won the state championship—and no one thought we'd be any good. We just finished in second place in the John Ehret tournament, and we had a long quiet bus ride home—because we all lived with some intimidation from Fitz. When we got back to the gym, he was pretty quiet in his demeanor and jingling the coins in his pocket, as he always would. He had our runner-up trophy in his hand. "You know what I think about second place?" he said. "Here's what I think about second place." And he slammed the trophy against the floor and we all flinched and covered our eyes, because these tiny shattered pieces were flying all over the place. The little man from the top of the trophy landed in the lap of the guy

next to me. I loved that moment. We took the little man
and put him up on top of the air conditioner. We touched
the little man on our way out of the locker room, before
every game. Second place: yeah, that wasn't our goal,
either. . . . I still think about Fitz. In moments when my
own discipline is slipping, I will have flashbacks of him.

The more I looked into it, the more mysterious
this new twist in Fitz's coaching career became. No
parent ever confronted Fitz directly. They did their
work behind his back. The closest to a direct complaint that I can tease from the parents I speak with
comes from a father of a current player. "You know
about what Fitz did to Peyton Manning, don't you?"
he said. Manning, now the quarterback of the Indi-
anapolis Colts, and MVP of the NFL, played basketball and baseball at Newman for Fitz. Fitz, the story
went, had benched Manning for skipping basketball
practice, and Manning had challenged him. They'd

had words, maybe even come to blows, and Manning had left the basketball team. And while he had continued to play baseball for Fitz, their relationship was widely taken as proof, by those who sought it, that Fitz was out of control. "You ought to read Peyton's book," the disgruntled father says. "It's all in there."

And it is. Written with his father, Archie, Peyton Manning's memoir is, understandably, mostly about football. But it isn't his high school football coach that Manning dwells on in his memoir: it's Fitz. He goes on for pages about his old baseball coach, and does indeed, in the end, reveal what Fitz did to him:

One of the things I had to learn growing up was toughness, because it doesn't seem to be something you can count on being born with. Dad says he may have told me, "Peyton, you have to stand up for this or that," but the resolve that gets it done is something you probably have to appreciate first in others. Coach Fitz was a major source for mine, and I'm grateful.

Of course you should never trust a memoir. And so I called Archie Manning, who laughed and said, "Fitz and Peyton had their issues. But I have a theory. The reason they locked horns is that they are exactly alike. Peyton's just as intense as Fitz is. But you should call Peyton and hear what he has to say." Peyton Manning might be the highest-paid player in pro football but, on the subject of Fitz, he has no sense of the value of his time. "As far as the respect and admiration I feel for the man," Manning said, "I couldn't put it into words. Just incredibly strong. For me, personally, he prepared me for so much of what I faced at the college and pro level. Unlike some coaches— for whom it's all about winning and losing—Coach Fitz was trying to make men out of people. I think he prepares you for life. And, if you want my opinion,

the people who are screwing up high school sports are the parents. The parents who want their son to be the next Michael Jordan. Or the parent who beats up the coach, or gets into a fight in the stands. Here's a coach who is so intense. Yet he's never laid a hand on anybody."

It was true. Fitz never laid a hand on anyone. He didn't need to. He had other ways of getting our attention.

IT had been nine months since I'd established, to my satisfaction, my heroic qualities. I was now pitching for the varsity, and we now had explicit training rules: no smoking, no drinking, no drugs, no staying out late. We signed a contract saying as much, but Fitz had too much of a talent for melodrama to leave our commitment to baseball so cut and dried. There were the written rules; and there were *the rules*. Over Easter vacation half of adolescent New Orleans decamped for the Florida beaches, where sex, along with a lot of other things, was unusually obtainable. Fitz forbade anyone who played for him from going to Florida and, to help them resist temptation, held early-morning practices every day. Once he discovered that two of our players had, in the dead of night, between morning practices, driven the eight hours to Florida and back. He herded us all into the locker room and said that while he couldn't prove his case, he knew that some of us had strayed from the path, and that he hoped the culprits got sand in an awkward spot where it would hurt for the rest of their lives. (He put it a bit more colorfully than that, and somewhere in New Orleans there are two forty-three-year-old men who flinch whenever they see a beach.)

Graduating from Babe Ruth to the varsity with only the slightest physical justification (I now resembled less a scoop of vanilla ice cream than a rounder Hobbit) meant coping with an out-of-control hormonal arms race. A few of our players had sprouted sideburns; but the enemy retaliated by growing terrifying little goatees and showing up at games with wives and, on one shocking occasion, children. I still had no muscles, and no facial hair, but I did have my own odor. I smelled, pretty much all the time, like Ben-Gay. I wore the stuff on my perpetually sore right shoulder and elbow. I wore it, also, on the bill of my cap, where Fitz had taught me to put it, to generate the grease for a spitball that might just compensate for my pathetic fastball. Everywhere I went that year, I emitted a vaguely medicinal vapor; and it is the smell of Ben-Gay I associate with what happened next.

What happened next is that, during Mardi Gras break, I left New Orleans with my parents for a week of vacation. I had thought that if I was a baseball success, and I was becoming one, that was enough. But it wasn't; success, to Fitz, was a process. Life as he led it, and expected us to lead it, had less to do with trophies than with sacrifice, in the name of some larger purpose: baseball. By missing a full week of practices over Mardi Gras, I had just violated some sacred, but unwritten, rule. Now I was back on the mound, a hunk of Ben-Gay drooping from the brim of my cap, struggling to relocate myself and my curveball. I didn't have the nerve to throw the spitter. I'd walked the first two batters I'd faced, and was pitching nervously to the third.

Ball two.

As I pitched I had an uneasy sensation—on bad days I can still feel it, like a bum knee—of having strayed from The Fitz Way. But I had no evidence of Fitz's displeasure; he hadn't said anything about the missed practices. Then his voice boomed out of our dugout.

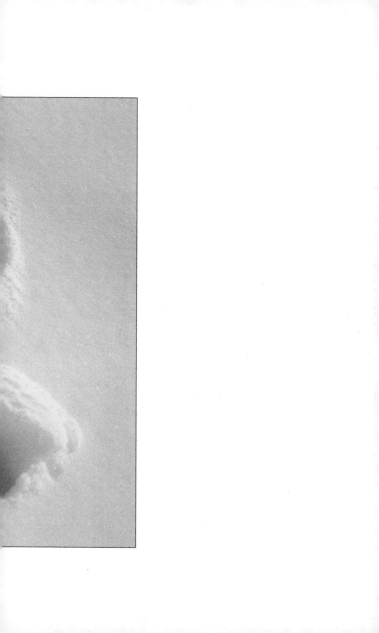

"Where was Michael Lewis during Mardi Gras?"

I did my best not to look over, but out of the corner of my eye I could see him. He was pacing the dugout. I threw another pitch.

Ball three.

"Everyone else was at practice. But where was Michael Lewis?"

I was now pitching with one eye on the catcher's mitt and the other on our dugout.

Ball four.

The bases were now loaded. Another guy in need of a shave came to the plate.

"I'll tell you where Michael Lewis was: skiing!"

Skiing, in 1976, for a fifteen-year-old New Orleanian, counted as an exotic activity. Being exposed as a vacation skier on a New Orleans baseball field in 1976 was as alarming as being accused of wearing pink silk underpants in a maximum security prison. Then and there, on the crabgrass of Slidell,

Louisiana, Coach Fitz packed into a single word what he usually required an entire speech to say: privilege corrupts. You were always doing what money could buy instead of what duty demanded. You were always *skiing*. As a *skier*, you developed a conviction, buttressed by your parents' money, that life was meant to be easy. That, when difficulty arose, you could just hire someone to deal with it. That nothing mattered so much that you should suffer for it.

But now, suddenly, something did matter so much that I should suffer for it: baseball. Or, more exactly: Fitz! The man was pouring his heart and soul into me, and demanding in return only that I pour myself into the game. He'd earned the right to holler at me whatever he wanted to holler. I got set to throw another pitch, in the general direction of the strike zone.

"Can someone please tell me why Michael Lewis thinks it's okay to leave town and go . . . and go . . . and go . . . ?"

Please, don't say skiing, I recall thinking, as the ball

left my hand. *Or, if you must say skiing, don't shout it.* Just then, the batter hit a sharp one-hopper back to the mound. I raised my glove to start the face-saving double play at the plate, but my ears were straining to catch Fitz's every word. And then, abruptly, his shouting stopped.

When I regained consciousness, I was on my back, blinking up at a hazy, not terribly remorseful Fitz. The baseball had broken my nose in five places. Oddly enough, I did not feel wronged. I felt, in an entirely new way, cared for. On the way to the hospital, to get my nose fixed, I told my mother that the next time the family went skiing—or anyplace else, for that matter—they'd be going without me. After the doctor pieced my nose back together, he told me that if I still wanted to play baseball I had to do it behind a mask. Grim as it all sounds, I don't believe I had ever been happier in my adolescent life. The rest of that season, when I walked out to the pitcher's

mound, I resembled a rounder Hobbit with a bird-cage on his face; but I'd never been so filled with a sense of purpose. Immediately, I had a new taste for staying after baseball practice, for extra work. I became, in truth, something of a zealot, and it didn't take long to figure out how much better my life could be if I applied this new zeal acquired on a baseball field to the rest of it. It was as if this baseball coach had reached inside me, found a rusty switch marked Turn On Before Attempting To Use, and flipped it.

Not long after that, the English teacher who also had the misfortune to experience me as a freshman held me after class to say that, by some happy miracle, I was not recognizably the same human being I'd been a year earlier. "What has happened?" she asked. It was hard to explain.

I HADN'T been to a Newman baseball game since I last played in one. On this sunny late-winter day, Fitz had arranged for his defending state champions to play a better team from a bigger school, twenty miles outside New Orleans. Fitz's hair had gone gray, and he was carrying a few more pounds, but he retained his chief attribute: the room still felt more pressurized simply because he was in it. He was a man who had become an idea, and he was able to seem as much like an idea as a man even when he was standing right in front of you. Which he was. Before an afternoon baseball game he tried to explain to me how he had become so routinely controversial. "I definitely have a penchant for crossing the line," he said, "and some parents definitely think I'm out of control." The biggest visible change in his coaching life was a thicker veneer of professionalism. His players now had fancy batting cages, better weight rooms, the latest training techniques, and scouting reports on opposing players. What they didn't have, most of them, was a meaningful relationship with their coach. "I can't get inside them anymore," he said. "They don't get it. But most kids don't get it. The trouble is every time I try the parents get in the way."

By "it" he did not mean the importance of winning or even, exactly, of trying hard. What he meant was neatly captured on a sheet of paper he held in his hand, which he intended to photocopy and hand out to his players, as the keynote for one of his sermons. The paper contained a quote from Lou Piniella, the legendary baseball manager: HE WILL NEVER BE A TOUGH COMPETITOR. HE DOESN'T KNOW HOW TO BE COMFORTABLE WITH BEING UNCOMFORTABLE. "It" was the importance of battling one's way through all the easy excuses life offered for giving up. Fitz had a gift for addressing this psychological problem, but he was no longer permitted to use it. "The trouble is," he said, "every time I try the parents get in the way." About these parents, he knows more than I ever imagined. Alcoholism, troubled marriages, overbearing fathers—he is disturbingly alert to problems in his players' home lives. (Did he know all this stuff about us?)

Fitz's office wasn't the office of a coach who wanted others to know of his many triumphs. There were no trophies or plaques, though he had won enough of them to fill five offices. Other than a few old newspaper clips about his four children, now grown, there were few mementos. What he did keep was books—lots of them. He was always something of a closet intellectual, though, as a boy, I was barely aware of this side of him. But I remember: when I first met him, he taught eighth-grade science and was working his way toward a PhD in biology. There were other clues that, as easily as he could be stereotyped as The Intense Coach, he had other dimen-

sions. He was a devoted father. His wife, Peggy, was so pretty she made us all blush; and, more to the point, she didn't seem to be the slightest bit intimidated by her husband. He had friends who didn't bite, and he even made small talk. But I'd paid no attention to any of this. All I knew was that he cared about the way we played a game in a way we'd never seen anyone care about anything. All I had wanted from him back then was his intensity. Now I simply wanted something less relevant, the truth.

"What really happened in your fight with Pete Maravich?" I asked him.

And he laughed. He never beat up Pete Maravich. (The truly brave thing he had done was ask his Tulane coach for the job of guarding Maravich.) And though he did appear with Maravich on the cover of *Sports Illustrated*, he was guarding him, not throttling him. He never chased around after Rusty Staub either. Why would he be chasing Rusty Staub? he wondered.

They'd gone to the same school. Fitz was an eighth grader when Staub was a senior. He never walked home after his high school team lost—they seldom lost—though he had, once, at Tulane. ("I got to the parish line and thought, hmm, is this really a good idea?") So where did they come from, these stories we told each other? They came from the imaginations of fourteen-year-old boys, in search of something even well-to-do parents couldn't provide.

Then I noticed: on one of his bookshelves Fitz still kept an old black-and-white photograph of Sean Tuohy leaping into Fitz's arms after their final, improbable state basketball championship. I asked him, "Do you remember the time that summer when you went out to the mound one too many times, all hell broke loose in the stands, and you had to pull Sean out of the game?"

"No."

"*No?*"

"That was a lifetime ago."

A moment that had prospered in my memory for thirty years was, for him, just one more forgettable piece of coaching history. I had been just another white rabbit he'd pulled out of a hat. But the wonder wasn't that the trick meant more to the white rabbit than to the magician; the wonder was that the magician was no longer permitted to look for white rabbits inside empty hats. When I asked Fitz how he'd adapted to parents sitting on his shoulder as he tried to coach their children, there was a hint of bitterness in his reply. "I've had to learn that you can't save everybody," he said.

"What do you mean 'save'?"

That gave him pause, and a new expression—of a man thinking about how what he said might sound if it was repeated. "I don't mean I can save their lives or their careers, or anything like that," he said. "I mean

that some of them will never understand the responsibility they have to their teams and themselves."

I had a different recollection of the sort of salvation he was aiming at. I recalled a man trying to give boys a sense that their lives could be something other than ordinary.

"I can't talk like that anymore," he said.

"Why not?"

"Look," he said. "All this is about a false sense of self-esteem. It's now bestowed on kids at birth. It's not earned. If I were to jump all over you today, you would be highly insulted and deeply offended. You would not get that I cared about you."

I never had any great sense of what Fitz made of the world outside his baseball program. Not much, I'd guess. He was running an organization that, like the Franciscan order or the Marine Corps, depended on a more difficult system of values than that of the greater society. In the corner of his office lay, haphaz-

ardly, an old stack of inspirational signs, hung by Fitz in the boys' locker room, and removed for the current renovation—the one that will leave the gym named for him. I picked up one and brushed away the dust: *What is to give light must endure burning*—Viktor Frankl.

He laughed. "I don't think we'll be putting that one back up."

Later, at the ballpark, a few of the fathers who had complained about Fitz clustered behind home plate. On the other end of the otherwise empty bleachers from them sat another man. His name was Stan Bleich, and he was a cardiologist who had grown up in Brooklyn. Both details were significant. He wasn't, like most of the dads, a lawyer. And he'd lived in New Orleans only twenty years, so by local standards he was an arriviste. An outsider. "I've had three kids go through Newman. I've thirty-nine school years of

Newman parent life," he says. "And I've never once called the headmaster."

That changed last summer. One of the fathers, upset about Fitz's speech to his son, called Stan to encourage him to join the group, and file a formal complaint. Instead, Stan went to see the headmaster and make the case for the defense. "The story had gotten so exaggerated," he says now. "One parent said, 'Fitz called my kid fat.' But all Fitz said to that kid was, 'You promised me you'd lose fifteen pounds and you gained ten.' " Bleich said the headmaster told him that, because of Fitz, the kids left with a bad taste in their mouths. "I said, wait a minute, shouldn't they leave with a bad taste in their mouths? They skipped practice. They didn't try. The game when Fitz missed his grandson's christening, three of the kids took off for Paris." Stan said Fitz reminded him of a college professor he had—and was grateful that he had.

"Ninety percent was not an A. One hundred percent was an A. Ninety percent was an F." He motions to the group of fathers on the other end of the bleachers. "A couple of those guys won't talk to me," he says, "because I defended Fitz. But what can I do? My goal in life is not for my son to play college ball. Fitz has made my kid a better person, not just a better athlete. He's taught him that if he works at it, anything he wants, it's there for him."

What was odd about this little speech—and, as the game began, became glaringly apparent—is that Stan Bleich's son was, far and away, the team's best player. At last count more than forty colleges were recruiting Jeremy Bleich to play baseball for them—and he was still only a junior. The question wasn't whether he would be able to play Division I college ball; the question was: would he skip college to sign with the Yankees out of high school? He was a sixteen-year-old left-handed pitcher with a good fastball, great command, a big league changeup, and charm to burn. He had no obvious baseball social deformity, other than his love for his coach, but that fact alone alienated him from his teammates. The first baseman has recently pelted the Bleich home with eggs. The older kids on the team poked fun at Jeremy, but, in keeping with the spirit of their insurrection, never directly. "I've never had anyone say anything to my face," Jeremy tells me later. "It's all behind my back. Like, last year, they started calling me 'J. Fitz.' I'm fifteen years old and the seniors are making fun of me. I had no idea how to deal with it. They don't like me because I work hard? Because I care about it? I'm like, I can't change that." He never knows exactly what the other players might be saying about him, but he knows what they say about Fitz: "They think his intensity is ridiculous." And maybe they do. Of course, one fringe benefit of laughing at intensity is

that it enables you to ignore the claims a new kind of seriousness makes upon you.

An invisible line ran from the parents' desire to minimize their children's discomfort to the choices the children make in their lives. A week later, two days before the start of their regular season, eight players got caught drinking. All but one of them—two team captains, two members of the school's honor committee—lied about it before confessing under duress. After he'd handed out the obligatory, school-sanctioned two-week suspensions to eight players, Fitz gathered the entire team for a sharp, little talk. Not two days ago he had the patience for a long sermon, about the dangers of getting a little too good at displacing responsibility. ("You're gonna lose. You're gonna have someone else to blame for it. But you're gonna lose. Is that what you want?") Now he had only the patience for a vivid threat: "I'm going to run you until you hate me." The first phone call, a few

hours later, came from the mother of the third baseman, who said her son had drank only "one sip of a
margarita," and so shouldn't be made to run. She was
followed by another father who wanted to know why
his son, the second baseman, wasn't starting at short-
stop instead.

THERE was always a question whether Fitz controlled his temper, or his temper controlled him, or
even if it mattered. In any case, the summer of 1976
had been especially uncomfortable. Fitz had entered
us in a better league, with bigger schools. Defeat followed listless defeat, until the night of this final Fitz
story. We had just lost by some truly spectacular
score. Twice at the end of the game he had shouted at
our base runners to slide, and, perhaps not seeing the

point, when down 15–2, in getting scraped, or even dirty, they'd gone in standing up. Afterward, at eleven o'clock or so, we piled off the bus and into the gym. Before we could undress, Fitz said, "We're going out back." Out back of the gym was a sorry excuse for a playing field. The dirt was packed as hard as asphalt and speckled with shell shards, glass, bottle caps, and god knows what else. Fitz lined us up behind first base and explained we were going to practice running to third. When we got there, we were to slide headfirst into the base. This, he said, would teach us to get down when he said to get down. Then he vanished into the darkness. A few moments later we heard his voice, from the general vicinity of third base. One by one, our players took off. In the beginning there was some grumbling, but before long the only sound was of Fitz, spotting a boy coming at him out of the darkness, shouting "Hit it!"

Over and over again we circled the bases, finishing

with a headfirst slide onto, in effect, concrete. We ran and slid on that evil field, until we bled and gasped for breath. The boy in front of me, a sophomore new to Fitz, began to cry. I remember thinking, absurdly, "you're too young for this." Finally, Fitz decided we'd had enough, and ordered us back inside. Back in the light we marveled at the evening's most visible consequence: ripped, muddy, and bloody uniforms. We undressed and began to throw them into the laundry baskets—until Fitz stopped us. "We're not washing them," he said. "Not until we win."

Well, we were never going to win. We were out of our league. For the next few weeks—seven games—we wore increasingly foul and bloody and torn uniforms. We lost our ability to see our own filth; our appearance could be measured only by its effect on others. In that small community of people who cared about high school baseball, word spread of this team that never bathed. People came to the ballpark just to

see us get off the bus. Opposing teams, at first amused, became alarmed, and then, I thought, just a tiny bit scared. You could see it in their eyes, the universal fear of the lunatic. *Heh, heh, heh*, those eyes said, nervously, *this is just a game, right?* The guys on the other teams came to the ballpark to play baseball—at which they just happened to be naturally superior. They played with one eye on the bar or the beach they were off to after the game. We alone were on this hellish quest for self-improvement.

After each loss we rode the bus back to the gym in silence. When we arrived, Fitz gave another of his sermons. They were always a little different but they never strayed far from a general theme: What It Means To Be A Man. What it meant to be a man was that you struggled against your natural instinct to run away from adversity. You battled. "You go to war with me, and I'll go to war with you," he loved to say. "Jump on my back." The effect of his words on the male adolescent mind was greatly enhanced by their delivery. It's funny that after all these years I can recall only snippets of what Fitz said, but I can recall, in slow motion, everything he broke. There was the orange water cooler, cracked with a single swing of an aluminum baseball bat. There was a large white wall clock that had hung in the Newman locker room for decades—until he busted it with a single throw of a catcher's mitt.

The breaking of things was a symptom; the disease was the sheer effort the man put into the job of making us better. He was always the first to arrive, and always the last to leave, and if any kid wanted to stay late for extra work, Fitz stayed with him. Before one game he became seriously ill. He climbed on the bus in a cold sweat. It was an hour's drive to the ballpark that day and he had the driver stop twice, on the highway, so he could get off and vomit. He remained sick right through the game, and all the way home.

When we arrived at the gym, he paused to vomit, then delivered yet another impassioned speech. A few nights later, after a game, in the middle of what must be the grubbiest losing streak in baseball history, I caught him walking. I was driving home, through a bad neighborhood, when I spotted him. Here he was, in one of America's murder capitals, inviting trouble. It was miles from the gym to his house, and he owned a car, yet he was hoofing it. What the hell is he doing? I thought, and then I realized: He's walking home! Just the way they said he'd done in high school, every time his team lost! It was as if he was doing penance for our sins.

And then something happened: we changed. We ceased to be embarrassed about our condition. We ceased, at least for a moment, to fear failure. We became, almost, a little proud. We were a bad baseball team united by a common conviction: *those other guys might be better than us, but there is no chance they could endure Coach Fitz.* The games became closer; the battles more fiercely fought. We were learning what it felt like to lay it all on the line. Those were no longer hollow words; they were a deep feeling. And finally, somehow, we won. No one who walked into our locker room as we danced around and hurled our uniforms into the washing machine, and listened to the speech Fitz gave about our fighting spirit, would have known they were looking at a team that now stood 1–12.

We listened to the man because he had something to tell us, and us alone. Not how to play baseball, though he did that better than anyone. Not how to win, though winning was wonderful. Not even how to sacrifice. He was teaching us something far more important: how to cope with the two greatest enemies of a well-lived life, fear and failure. To make the lesson stick, he made sure we encountered enough of both. What he knew—and I'm not sure he'd ever

consciously thought it, but he knew it all the same—
was that we'd never conquer the weaknesses within
ourselves. We'd never drive the worst of ourselves
away for good. We'd never win. The only glory to be
had would be in the quality of the struggle.

I never could have explained at the time what he
had done for me, but I felt it in my bones all the
same. When I came home one day my senior year, and
found the letter saying that, somewhat improbably, I
had been admitted to Princeton University, I ran
right back to school to tell Coach Fitz. Then I grew up.

I'D gone back to New Orleans again. The *Times-
Picayune* had just picked the Newman Greenies to win
another state championship. The only hitch is that
they no longer had nine eligible ballplayers. The

drinking suspensions had made them less than a baseball team. It was a glorious Saturday afternoon and the team was meant to be playing a game, but the game had been forfeited. Fitz said nothing to the players about the canceled games but instead took them out onto the hard field out back. He began by hitting ground balls to the infielders and fly balls to the outfielders. His face had a waxen pallor, he was running a fever, and he was not, frankly, in the sweetest of moods. He was under the impression that he was now completely hamstrung—that if he did anything approaching what he'd like to do, "I'll be in the headmaster's office on Monday morning."

Nevertheless, a kind of tension built—what would he do this time? what *could* he do?—until finally he called the team in to home plate. On the hard field in front of him, only a few yards from the place where, years ago, another group of teenaged boys slid until

they hurt, they formed their usual semicircle. Fitz has a tone perhaps best described as unnervingly pleasant: it's pleasant because it's calm; it's unnerving because he's not. In this special tone of his, he opened with one of Aesop's fables. The fable was about a boy who hurled rocks into a pond, until a frog rises up and asks him to stop. "No," says the boy. "It's fun." "And the frog says," said Fitz, " 'what's fun for you is death to me.' " Before anyone could wonder how that frog might apply to a baseball team, Fitz told them: "That's how I feel about you right now. You are like that boy. You all are all about fun." His tone remained even, but it was not the evenness of a still pond. It was the evenness of a pot of water just before the fire beneath it is turned up. Sure enough, a minute into the talk, his voice began to simmer:

When are you consciously going to start dealing with the fact that this is a competitive situation? I mean, you are almost a *recreational* baseball team. The trouble is you don't play in a recreational league. You play serious, competitive interscholastic baseball. That means the other guy isn't out for recreation. He wants to strike you out. He wants to *embarrass* you . . . until your eyeballs roll over.

The boys were paying attention now. The man was born to drill holes into thick skulls, and shout directly into the adolescent brain. I was as riveted by his performance as I'd been twenty-five years ago—which was good, as he was coming to his point.

One of the goodies about athletics is you get to find out if you can stretch. *If you can get better.* But you got to push. And you guys don't even push to get through the day. You put more effort into parties than you do into this team.

Then he cited several examples of parties into which his baseball players had put great effort. For a man with such overt contempt for parties, he was distressingly well informed about their details—including the fact that, at some, the parents provided the booze.

I know about parents. I know how much they love to say "I pay fourteen thousand dollars in tuition and so my little boy deserves to play." No way. You *earn* the right to play. I had a mom and dad too, you know. I loved my mom and dad. My dad didn't understand much about athletics, and so he didn't always *get* it. You have to make that distinction at some point. At some point you have to stand up and be a man and say, "This is how I'm going to do it. This is how I'm going to approach it." When is the last time any of you guys did that?

No. For you, it's all "fun." Well, it's not all fun. Some days it's work.

Then he wrapped it up, with a quote from Mark Twain about how the difference between animals and people—the ability to think—is diminished by people's refusal to think. Aesop to Mark Twain, with a baseball digression and a lesson on self-weaning: the whole thing required five minutes.

And then his mood shifted completely. The kids clambered to their feet, and followed their coach back to baseball practice. That coach faced the most deeply entrenched attitude problem in his players in thirty-one years. His wife, Peggy, had hinted to me that, for the first time, Fitz was thinking about giving up coaching altogether. He faced a climate of opinion—created by well-intentioned parents, abetted by a school more subservient than ever to its paying customers—that made it nearly impossible for him to change those attitudes. He faced, in short, a world trying to stop him from making his miracles. And on top of it all, he had the flu. It counted as the lowest moment in his career as a baseball coach. Unfairly, I took that moment to ask him: "Do you really think there's any hope for this team?" The question startled him into a new freshness. He was alive, awake, almost well again. "*Always*," he said. "You never give up on a team. Just like you never give up on a kid." Then he pauses. "But it's going to take some work."

And that's how I left him. Largely unchanged. No longer, sadly, my baseball coach. Instead, the kind of person who might one day coach my children. And when I think of that, I become aware of a new fear: that my children might never meet up with their Fitz. Or that they will, and their father will fail to understand what he's up to.

The author, age sixteen, pitching for the Newman Greenies.

PHOTO CREDITS